Chancellor of Germany 1949- 2024

Jan Driessen

Published by Jan Dierssen, 2024.

While every precaution has been taken in the preparation of this book, the publisher assumes no responsibility for errors or omissions, or for damages resulting from the use of the information contained herein.

CHANCELLOR OF GERMANY 1949- 2024

First edition. January 5, 2024.

Copyright © 2024 Jan Driessen.

ISBN: 979-8223796893

Written by Jan Driessen.

Table of Contents

Chapter

Chapter 1: Introduction

1 1: Introduction

- 1.1 Tasks of the Federal Chancellor: The role of the head of government in Germany

- 1.2 Appointment and election of the Federal Chancellor: How is the Federal Chancellor elected in Germany?

- 1.3 The Political Context of the Elections: Factors Influencing the Outcome

Chapter 2: Konrad Adenauer (1949-1963)

Chapter 3: Ludwig Erhard (1963-1966)

Chapter 4: Willy Brandt (1969-1974)

Chapter 5: Helmut Schmidt (1974-1982)

Capitel 6: Helmut Kohl (1982-1998)

Chapter 7: Gerhard Schröder (1998-2005)

- 7.1 Gerhard Schröder: Biography - A Life Full of Political Ups and Downs

- 7.2 Gerhard Schröder: The election as Chancellor

- 7.3 Gerhard Schröder: The role in his party (SPD)

- *7.4 Gerhard Schröder: Agenda 2010 and economic reforms*

- 7.5 Gerhard Schröder: International Politics and Criticism

Chapter 8: Angela Merkel (2005-2021)

Chapter 9: Olaf Scholz (since 2021)

JAN DRIESSEN

l 1: Introduction

• 1.1 Tasks of the Federal Chancellor: The role of the head of government in Germany

The Federal Chancellor is the head of government of Germany and has a variety of tasks. One of its most important tasks is to implement the decisions of the Bundestag and to conduct government business. The Chancellor is also the face of the German government and represents the country at the international level.

As head of government of the Federal Republic of Germany, the Federal Chancellor has many important tasks. In addition to its representative tasks, such as representing Germany at home and abroad, it also has the appointment and dismissal of federal ministers. The Federal Chancellor is thus also the Chairman of the Federal Cabinet and chairs the weekly Cabinet meetings.

In the Federal Republic of Germany, the Federal Chancellor plays a key role in the political landscape. He is not only the head of the federal government, but also the most important political decision-maker in the country. His decisions have far-reaching consequences for society as a whole. In order to be able to make these decisions, the Chancellor must always be up to date and work closely with his cabinet.

For many people, the Federal Chancellor is an important political figure who stands for stability and continuity in the Federal Republic of Germany. His ability to make political decisions and represent the country's interests is crucial for Germany's future.

Another important task of the Federal Chancellor is to represent Germany's interests at the international level and to maintain relations with other countries. In this context, the Federal Chancellor often travels abroad and meets with other heads of state and government to discuss political issues and find common solutions.

However, the Chancellor represents Germany's interests not only on official state visits, but also at international conferences and summits. This often involves issues such as trade relations, climate protection, peace and security.

Close cooperation between states is essential to successfully tackle global challenges such as climate change or the fight against poverty and hunger. In this context, the Federal Chancellor plays an important role as a mediator and ambassador of Germany.

By exchanging ideas with other heads of state and government as well as international organisations, new ideas and solutions can be developed to make the world a better place. In this sense, the Chancellor is an important player on the global stage and helps to ensure that Germany also has a strong voice internationally.

It is important to emphasize that the Chancellor does not have absolute power and that his decisions can be reviewed by the Bundestag and other political institutions. This separation of powers is an important part of the German political system and guarantees that no single person has too much power.

Nevertheless, the Chancellor is a key figure in German politics and his decisions often have far-reaching effects on the country and its citizens. The Chancellor is the face of Germany in the world and represents the country on the international stage. It is therefore important that the Chancellor makes his decisions wisely and always keeps the well-being of the country and its citizens in mind.

For more information on the office of the Federal Chancellor and his role in German politics, please visit the official website of the Federal Government: https://www.bundesregierung.de/breg-de/bundeskanzleramt

• 1.2 Appointment and election of the Federal Chancellor: How is the Federal Chancellor elected in Germany?

In Germany, the Federal Chancellor is appointed by the Federal President. The Federal Chancellor is elected by the Bundestag and appointed by the Federal President. The Federal President appoints the candidate who receives the majority of the votes in the Bundestag as Federal Chancellor.

This is a very important procedure that concerns the political leadership of our country. The Chancellor is the highest-ranking government official in Germany and has an important role in shaping our country's political agenda.

There are many factors that need to be taken into account when choosing a Federal Chancellor. Political parties must agree on a candidate who is the best choice for the country. The candidate must be able to understand and represent the needs of the people.

It is also important to note that the Chancellor does not govern alone. He or she must work closely with other government officials to make effective policy decisions. Strong leadership and a good team are the keys to success.

In this context, it is important to emphasise that political decisions in Germany are made on a democratic basis. The Bundestag is the most important body for political decisions, and the elections are the way in which the people cast their votes.

Overall, the appointment of the Chancellor is an important process that needs to be carefully considered. It is important that we all remember that as citizens of our country, we can play an important role in shaping the political agenda.

The appointment of the Federal Chancellor is an important step in the formation of a German government. The Federal Chancellor is the head of government of the Federal Republic of Germany and plays a central role in German politics. The election of the Federal Chancellor is a complex process that consists of several steps.

The parties in the Bundestag play an important role in the election of the Federal Chancellor. They propose candidates, who are then elected by the Bundestag. It is important that the candidate receives a majority of the votes in the Bundestag. This is the only way to appoint the candidate as Federal Chancellor.

The Federal President has a decisive role in the appointment of the Federal Chancellor. After the election of the Federal Chancellor by the Bundestag, the candidate is appointed by the Federal President. The candidate who receives the most votes is appointed Chancellor.

Further information on the appointment of the Federal Chancellor can be found on the official website of the Federal Chancellery: https://www.bundeskanzleramt.de/Webs/BK/DE/Bundeskanzleramt/ AufgabenUndFunktionen/ErnennungBundeskanzler/ ernennungbundeskanzler-node.html

Further information on the formation of a government in Germany can be found on the website of the German Bundestag: https://www.bundestag.de/ parlament/aufgaben/rechte-und-pflichten/gesetzgebung/parlamentarische-beratungen/regierungsbildung-207880.

• 1.3 The Political Context of the Elections: Factors Influencing the Outcome

Politics is not just about who has the best arguments or who gets the most votes. It is also about the political context in which elections take place. This context encompasses a variety of factors that can influence the outcome of the election.

Factors influencing the outcome of the election include the political mood in the country, voter turnout, the campaign strategy of the parties and candidates, and media coverage. But that's not all. There are also many other factors that can influence the outcome of the election.

For example, the political landscape and events in the weeks and months leading up to the election can play a crucial role. For example, if there is a major scandal within a party or an important political issue comes into the focus of the media, this can influence the election.

The personality of the candidates and their ability to persuade voters can also have a big impact. If a candidate has a strong personality and is able to communicate their message effectively, it can make a big difference.

Last but not least, social media are also playing an increasingly important role in election campaigns. Through targeted advertising and campaigns, parties and candidates can try to influence public opinion and win over voters.

So, it's important to keep an eye on all the factors to gain a better understanding of the political landscape and the outcome of the election.

It is important that voters inform themselves about the political context before making their voting decision. This is the only way they can ensure that their voice is actually heard and that they have an impact on the political landscape.

For more information on the political context of the elections, please visit the following website: https://www.bundeswahlleiter.de/info/presse/mitteilungen/bundestagswahl-2017/02-17-wahlberechtigte.html

Chapter 2: Konrad Adenauer (1949-1963)

• 2.1 Konrad Adenauer: Biography

Konrad Adenauer was one of the most important German politicians of the 20th century. As the first German Chancellor after the Second World War, he had a decisive influence on Germany's post-war history. Adenauer was also one of the founding fathers of the European Union and campaigned for European unification throughout his life.

Konrad Adenauer was born in Cologne on 5 January 1876 and studied law, history and political science. From a young age, he joined the Centre Party and was committed to the interests of the Catholic Church. As Lord Mayor of Cologne from 1917 to 1933, he campaigned for the reconstruction of the city after the First World War and made a name for himself as a successful local politician.

However, Adenauer was successful not only as Lord Mayor of Cologne, but also as the first Chancellor of the Federal Republic of Germany, which he ruled from 1949 to 1963. During this time, he promoted the reconstruction of Germany and promoted European integration.

Adenauer was a visionary politician who recognized the importance of a united Europe and advocated close cooperation between European countries. His efforts were instrumental in making Germany an important member of the international community after the Second World War.

Today, numerous monuments and street names throughout Germany commemorate Konrad Adenauer, who went down in history as one of the most important German politicians of the 20th century.

After World War II, Adenauer was elected the first Chancellor of the Federal Republic of Germany. In this position, he worked for the reconstruction of the country and the integration of Germany into the Western world. Thanks to his leadership and vision, Germany was able to experience a rapid economic recovery after the war.

Adenauer was also instrumental in the founding of the European Coal and Steel Community, which later became the European Union. His commitment to European integration was of great importance for the future of Germany and Europe. Adenauer was a great supporter of the German-French friendship, which is regarded as the engine of European unification.

Adenauer was a wise and experienced statesman who dedicated his life to the betterment of Germany and Europe. His legacy will always be remembered and his work has left a lasting mark on history. If you want to know more about Adenauer and his achievements, you can do so on the following website: https://www.konrad-adenauer.de/wer-wir-sind/konrad-adenauer-stiftung/.

Adenauer was a man with a clear vision and a strong will. His political legacy continues to have an impact on Germany and Europe to this day.

• 2.2 Konrad Adenauer: The election as Chancellor

The election of Chancellor in 1949 was a historic moment for Germany. Finally, the country had the opportunity to have a democratically elected government. Konrad Adenauer was elected as the first Chancellor of the Federal Republic of Germany and laid the foundation for one of the most successful periods of government in German history.

Under his leadership, the country's economy was rebuilt and important steps were taken to reintegrate Germany into the international community. Adenauer was a visionary and worked hard to build a strong and stable Federal Republic of Germany based on the core values of democracy and respect for human rights.

Thanks to his work, Germany now has a stable democracy and one of the strongest economies in the world. We should always remember how important it is to have a strong and democratic government that is committed to the well-being of its people.

Adenauer was a conservative politician who stood up for Germany's interests and wanted to improve relations with other countries. Under his leadership, the economy was rebuilt and Germany's integration into the Western world was advanced.

Konrad Adenauer was the first Chancellor of the Federal Republic of Germany and ruled the country from 1949 to 1963. He was a man of great stature and political skill. Adenauer had a vision of a strong and united Germany living in peace and freedom with its neighbors.

Adenauer was committed to European unification and was an important architect of the European unification process. He recognized that closer cooperation between European countries was necessary to ensure peace and stability in Europe.

Under Adenauer's leadership, Germany's economy was rebuilt and modernized. He promoted the reconstruction of industry and trade, which led to an economic boom. Adenauer also contributed to Germany's integration into the Western world by improving relations with the U.S. and other Western countries.

Overall, Adenauer was an important statesman who made a great contribution to the development of Germany and Europe. His legacy is still felt today and his vision of a united Europe lives on.

But despite his successes, there were also critics and opponents. Some accused him of being a "spiritual charlatan" who influenced the Catholic Church in Germany too much. But Adenauer was not deterred and remained true to his convictions.

Today, Adenauer is regarded as one of the most important politicians in German history. His vision and deeds have made Germany a strong and successful country that is respected in the world.

More information about Konrad Adenauer and his political achievements can be found at the following link: https://www.konrad-adenauer.de/

• 2.3 Konrad Adenauer: The role in his party (CDU)

Konrad Adenauer, the first Chancellor of the Federal Republic of Germany, was an important and influential politician of his time. But what was his role in his party, the CDU?

Adenauer was one of the founding members of the Christian Democratic Union (CDU) and had a great influence on the party. However, his political career began long before he co-founded the CDU. Konrad Adenauer was already a member of the Cologne city council in 1906 and later mayor of the city.

When he was finally elected chairman of the CDU in 1950, he had a decisive influence on the political orientation of the party. Adenauer was an advocate of ties with the West and advocated close ties with the United States. He is considered one of the architects of European integration and was a staunch supporter of the creation of the European Coal and Steel Community (ECSC), which later became the European Union (EU).

Adenauer was also an important player in German reunification. He campaigned for a rapprochement with the former GDR and supported the Ostpolitik of his successor Willy Brandt.

Despite his many successes and achievements, Adenauer was also controversial. Critics accused him of having an authoritarian leadership style and being too close to the Catholic clergy. But its importance for Germany's post-war history and European integration cannot be denied.

Further information on Konrad Adenauer and his political work can be found on the official website of the Konrad Adenauer Foundation: https://www.kas.de/de/home

Under Adenauer's leadership, the CDU developed into one of the most important political forces in Germany. He advocated a strong and stable economy and pursued a policy of ties to the West, which was intended to bind Germany closely to the Western states.

Adenauer was also an advocate of European unification and advocated close cooperation between European states. He was instrumental in the creation of the European Economic Community (EEC), which later became the European Union.

Although Adenauer was often referred to as the "Father of the Nation", he was not without controversy. Some critics accused him of being authoritarian and abusing his position of power in the party and the state. Nevertheless, Adenauer remains one of the most important personalities in German history to this day.

His influence on the founding of the Federal Republic of Germany is undisputed. Adenauer was the first Chancellor of the young republic and played a decisive role in setting the course for the new democracy. He campaigned for the reconstruction of Germany after the Second World War and campaigned strongly for Germany's integration into the Western community of states.

Adenauer's role in strengthening relations with other countries is also undisputed. In particular, his friendship with French President Charles de Gaulle contributed significantly to reconciliation between Germany and France. Adenauer and de Gaulle agreed that close cooperation between Germany and France was essential for peace in Europe. Adenauer's efforts to establish closer cooperation with the United States and other European states were also of great importance for the Federal Republic of Germany and the region as a whole.

If you would like to learn more about Adenauer's life and work, I recommend that you take a look at the official website of the Konrad Adenauer Foundation: https://www.kas.de/de/themen/konrad-adenauer. Here you will find a wealth of information and materials on Adenauer's political legacy.

Further information on Konrad Adenauer and his role in the CDU can be found here: https://www.konrad-adenauer.de/kas/geschichte/

• 2.4 Konrad Adenauer: Key moments and political decisions that shaped Germany

Konrad Adenauer was one of the most important German politicians of the 20th century. As the first Chancellor of the Federal Republic of Germany, he made a significant contribution to the country's political and economic stabilization after the Second World War and to its leading role in Europe.

A key moment in Adenauer's term of office was the signing of the Elysée Treaty in 1963. This treaty between Germany and France laid the foundation for close cooperation and friendship between the two countries, which is still of great importance today. Without a doubt, this treaty was a significant milestone in the history of Europe and helped to improve political relations between Germany and France.

The Élysée Treaty has had not only political but also cultural implications. He has promoted exchanges between the two countries in the fields of art, music, literature and sports. This has helped to strengthen the understanding and bond between the two countries.

Today, almost 60 years after the signing of the Elysée Treaty, the friendship between Germany and France remains strong. The two countries are working closely together to address Europe's political and economic challenges. It is important that we remember the importance of the Elysée Treaty and continue to cultivate this friendship in order to build a strong and united European Union.

Another important political moment in German history was Adenauer's decision to admit Germany to NATO, thus creating close ties with the United States. This decision had far-reaching implications for German foreign policy and contributed to Germany's re-recognition as a sovereign state after World War II.

By becoming a member of NATO, Germany was able to ensure its security and defence while at the same time establishing close relations with other member countries. These relations have been and continue to be of great importance for German foreign policy and have contributed to Germany's leading role in Europe today.

However, the decision to join NATO was not without controversy. Some critics feared that Germany could become too dependent on the U.S. and that this would affect relations with other countries. Nevertheless, the decision proved to be the right one, and Germany was able to pursue a stable and successful foreign policy in the decades that followed.

More information on this topic can be found on NATO's official website: https://www.nato.int/cps/de/natohq/topics_49170.htm

However, Adenauer's political career was also marked by controversy. Critics accused him of being a conservative hardliner who focused too much on the United States and too little on rapprochement with the Soviet Union. Others criticized his authoritarian leadership and his role in the passage of the Emergency Law.

Despite these controversies, Adenauer is now regarded as one of the most important German politicians of the 20th century. His political legacy continues to have an impact on German politics and society to this day.

• 2.5 Konrad Adenauer: Criticism and Controversies - A Critical View

Konrad Adenauer is considered one of the most important political figures in German history. However, he was also controversial and had to take criticism during his tenure as Chancellor.

One of Adenauer's most controversial decisions was undoubtedly his approval of the construction of the Berlin Wall in 1961. This decision was seen by many as a betrayal of the ideals of freedom and democracy. Adenauer, the first Chancellor of the Federal Republic of Germany, justified his approval by saying that he did not want to jeopardize the unity of Germany.

The Berlin Wall, which divided the city until 1989, was a symbol of the division of Germany and the Cold War. Many people, especially in the West, saw the construction of the wall as an inhumane act that separated people from their families and friends and restricted the freedom of citizens.

Despite criticism of his decision to build the Berlin Wall, Adenauer is widely regarded as one of the most important German politicians of the 20th century. His political influence has had a lasting impact on Germany and Europe. If you would like to learn more about Adenauer's life and work, you can find out more on the following website: https://www.konrad-adenauer.de/

Another point of criticism of Adenauer was his attitude towards the former National Socialists. Many accused him of not doing enough to counter the influence of the former Nazis in politics. However, Adenauer himself was of the opinion that a new beginning in politics was only possible with the participation of former National Socialists.

The topic of former National Socialists in politics is still a controversial topic today. Some argue that the past of the former Nazis disqualifies them, while others argue that they have the right to work in politics if they repent of their past and change. It's a difficult topic that evokes a lot of mixed opinions.

However, it is important to keep in mind that Germany went through a difficult time after World War II. There were many challenges that had to be overcome, and Adenauer had to make difficult decisions to rebuild the country. Although his decisions were not supported by everyone, his efforts to lead the country into a better future should be acknowledged.

For more information on this topic, please refer to the following page: https://de.wikipedia.org/wiki/Konrad_Adenauer

Despite these controversies, Konrad Adenauer remains an important part of German history and contributed significantly to the development of the Federal Republic of Germany.

Chapter 3: Ludwig Erhard (1963-1966)

- ## 3.1 Ludwig Erhard: Biography - The Father of the Economic Miracle

Ludwig Erhard was undoubtedly one of the most important German politicians of the 20th century. He was born on 4 February 1897 in Fürth and died on 5 May 1977 in Bonn. Erhard was a German politician of the Christian Democratic Union (CDU) and Federal Minister of Economics from 1949 to 1963.

Erhard had a clear vision for Germany: he wanted every citizen to be able to live in prosperity. His policy of "prosperity for all" was groundbreaking and made Germany one of the most successful economic nations in the world. Under Erhard's leadership, Germany was able to recover from the horrors of war and become a strong and stable economic power.

Erhard was a man of principles and convictions. He believed in the market economy and in the freedom of the individual to shape his life in a self-determined way. However, he was also a man of vision and a sense of responsibility. He knew how to use the forces of the market to promote the well-being of all citizens.

It is no wonder that Erhard is considered the "father of the economic miracle" in Germany. His legacy lives on in the German economy to this day and will continue to be an important part of Germany's success in the future.

Erhard became known for his free-market policies and his rejection of state intervention in the economy. His concept of the social market economy stood for a combination of free market economy and social justice. Erhard was a great advocate of the free market economy and believed that the state should stay out of economic affairs.

His policies were not without controversy and he was often described by critics as cold-hearted and anti-social. But Erhard remained convinced that the prosperity of society can best be achieved through a free market economy and individual freedom.

More information about Ludwig Erhard can be found on his official website: https://www.ludwig-erhard.de/

• 3.2 Ludwig Erhard: The election as Chancellor

In 1963, Ludwig Erhard was elected Federal Chancellor. Erhard, an economist and member of the Christian Democratic Union (CDU), had previously served as Minister of Economic Affairs and was instrumental in Germany's economic recovery after World War II.

Erhard's policy of the social market economy undoubtedly contributed to Germany's unprecedented economic boom in the 1950s and 1960s. Under his leadership, Germany became one of the world's leading economies. Erhard set the course for Germany's economic success and laid the foundations for Germany's current economic structure.

The social market economy has proven to be a successful economic model that not only creates prosperity for the general public, but also promotes social justice. Erhard stood up for the interests of workers and employers alike and thus promoted a balanced economy.

Today, more than 60 years after the introduction of the social market economy, Germany is still one of the leading economies in the world. The principles of the social market economy are still an important part of German economic policy and have helped Germany to remain successful in today's globalized world. Germany is a prime example of how sensible economic policies can lead to sustainable economic growth.

Source: Federal Agency for Civic Education[1]

The election as Chancellor was an important moment in German history and set the course for the future of the country. If you would like to learn more about Ludwig Erhard and his policies, please visit the following website: https://www.bundeskanzlerin.de/bkin-de/geschichte/alle-bundeskanzler/ludwig-erhard.

• 3.3 Ludwig Erhard: The role in his party (CDU)

---

1. https://www.bpb.de/nachschlagen/lexika/das-junge-politik-lexikon/182189/soziale-marktwirtschaft

Ludwig Erhard was an important politician and economist in the Federal Republic of Germany. He is considered one of the fathers of the German economic miracle and was a member of the German Bundestag from 1949 to 1963. As a member of the CDU, he played an important role in the party and contributed significantly to Germany's economic recovery after World War II.

Erhard always held fast to his convictions and vehemently championed his political goals. As Minister of Economic Affairs and later as Chancellor of Germany in the 1960s, he shaped the country's economic policy and made a significant contribution to the economic miracle. In doing so, he also accepted uncomfortable decisions if he was convinced that they would contribute to the well-being of the country.

Erhard's reforms, such as the introduction of the social market economy, the easing of price and wage controls, and the reduction of taxes and duties, contributed significantly to Germany's development into one of the leading economic powers after the Second World War. His achievements as Minister of Economic Affairs and Federal Chancellor remain unforgotten and are still regarded by many economists and politicians as exemplary for successful economic policy.

If you would like to learn more about Ludwig Erhard, you can find detailed information about his life and work on the official website of the Konrad Adenauer Foundation: https://www.kas.de/de/web/geschichte-der-cdu/personen/biogramm-detail/-/content/ludwig-erhard-1.

If you would like to learn more about Ludwig Erhard, you can find out more on the official website of the Ludwig Erhard Foundation: https://www.ludwig-erhard.de/. Here you will find a lot of interesting information and materials about this important German politician and business leader.

• 3.4 Ludwig Erhard: Economic Policy and Reforms

Ludwig Erhard was an eminent German economist and politician. He is considered one of the fathers of the post-war economic miracle and was Chancellor of the Federal Republic of Germany from 1963 to 1966.

Erhard's economic policy ideas were shaped by the conviction that a free market and a social market economy are the key to economic success. He was a visionary thinker who recognized the potential of a free market economy and fought for its implementation.

Through his reforms and economic policy visions, Ludwig Erhard contributed to Germany's rise to become one of the world's leading economies in the 1950s and 1960s. His ideas and measures laid the foundation for the economic miracle that Germany experienced during this time.

Erhard's insights and policy decisions were groundbreaking for many other countries that turned to Germany to reform their own economies. Erhard's legacy lives on to this day and has had a significant impact on the economic development of Germany and Europe.

Here is a link to more information about Ludwig Erhard: [https://www.bundeskanzlerin.de/bkin-de/geschichte/amt-und-institution/ bundeskanzler-seit-1949/ludwig-erhard-136740]

Let's talk about Ludwig Erhard. Among other things, Erhard carried out the currency reform of 1948 and campaigned for the dismantling of trade barriers. His political decisions contributed to Germany's enormous economic boom in the post-war period. Erhard's economic policies were an important factor in the success of the so-called "economic miracle" in the 1950s.

Erhard was a man with an impressive career. He studied economics and later received his doctorate in this field. He worked in various positions in the public sector before finally being appointed Minister of Economic Affairs in the Federal Government. Erhard was known for his liberal economic policies and his belief that the market offered the best solution to economic problems.

Despite his successes, Erhard also had his critics. Some argued that his policies led to an unequal distribution of wealth. Others criticized his rejection of unions and his support of employers. Nevertheless, Erhard remains one of the most important figures in German economic history and is often referred to as the father of the German economic miracle.

You can find out more about Ludwig Erhard and his economic policy on the official website of the Konrad Adenauer Foundation: https://www.kas.de/de/themen/dossier-ludwig-erhard.

• 3.5 Ludwig Erhard: Challenges and Failures

Ludwig Erhard was one of the most influential politicians of post-war Germany. As Federal Minister for Economic Affairs and later as Federal Chancellor, he made a significant contribution to Germany's economic development. Today, he is considered one of the fathers of the "economic miracle" and one of the architects of the social market economy.

But despite his great successes, Erhard also had to deal with challenges and setbacks. In particular, his controversial decision to freeze wages in the Federal Republic of Germany led to fierce protests and criticism from trade unions and employees.

Erhard's failure as chancellor in 1966 is often attributed to his controversial economic policies. But personal factors also played a role. His health was already fragile at the beginning of his term of office, which limited him in the performance of his duties. He was also unable to adapt quickly enough to the changing political landscape.

Another factor that may have contributed to Erhard's failure was his inability to make political compromises and form alliances. However, it is also important to emphasize that Erhard was also able to achieve some important successes during his term of office, such as the introduction of VAT or the improvement of relations with the USA.

Erhard's failure as Chancellor is an important event in German history and continues to have an impact on the country's politics to this day. If you want to learn more about Ludwig Erhard and his political career, I recommend taking a look at the official website of the Konrad Adenauer Foundation: https://www.kas.de/de/web/geschichte-der-cdu/personen/biogramm-detail/-/content/ludwig-erhard-v1

Despite his mistakes and weaknesses, however, Ludwig Erhard remains one of the most important figures in German history. His legacy lives on today in the social market economy and in Germany's economic strength.

Chapter 4: Willy Brandt (1969-1974)

- **4.1 Willy Brandt: Biography - The Life of a Great Statesman**

Willy Brandt was undoubtedly one of the most important statesmen in German history. His life and work are still of great importance for the Federal Republic of Germany and beyond. As the first Social Democratic Chancellor of the Federal Republic of Germany, he had a significant influence on the development of German politics and society.

Willy Brandt was born Herbert Ernst Karl Frahm on 18 December 1913 in Lübeck. In the years leading up to World War II, he fought against National Socialism and eventually had to go into exile. After his return to Germany, he was elected chairman of the SPD and later Governing Mayor of Berlin.

As Chancellor, he championed the policy of détente, which led to rapprochement between East and West. For his efforts, he was awarded the Nobel Peace Prize in 1971. His political legacy can still be felt today and has made a significant contribution to making Germany a strong and stable democracy.

You can find out more about the life of Willy Brandt in this biography[1].

- **4.2 Willy Brandt: The election as Federal Chancellor**

Willy Brandt was one of the most important politicians of the Federal Republic of Germany. He was the first Social Democratic Chancellor after the Konrad Adenauer era and had a decisive influence on the politics of the Federal Republic of Germany in the 1970s.

On 21 October 1969, Willy Brandt was elected Chancellor and formed a coalition government of the SPD and FDP. Brandt's chancellorship was marked by numerous domestic and foreign policy challenges, including Ostpolitik and the policy of détente during the Cold War.

---

1. https://www.bundeskanzler-willy-brandt-stiftung.de/willy-brandt/biografie/

Brandt pursued a new Ostpolitik aimed at improving relations with the Soviet Union and other Eastern Bloc countries. This led, among other things, to the signing of the Moscow Treaties in 1970 and the Warsaw Treaties in 1970/71. These treaties were an important step towards improving relations between East and West and easing tensions during the Cold War.

However, Brandt's chancellorship was also marked by internal challenges, such as the student movement and the terrorism of the RAF. During this period, important reforms were also carried out, such as the introduction of child benefit and the reform of divorce law.

Overall, Brandt's chancellorship was a time of change and challenges, but also of opportunities and improvement in relations between East and West.

As a charismatic orator and diplomat, Brandt enjoyed a high reputation worldwide. His policy of change and détente contributed significantly to the improvement of relations between East and West.

More information about Willy Brandt and his political career can be found at https://de.wikipedia.org/wiki/Willy_Brandt.

• 4.3 Willy Brandt: The role in his party (SPD)

Willy Brandt, born Herbert Frahm, was an important German politician. He was the fourth Chancellor of the Federal Republic of Germany from 1969 to 1974. But before he became chancellor, he played an important role in his party, the Social Democratic Party of Germany (SPD).

Brandt joined the SPD in 1930 and was active in the resistance against National Socialism during the Weimar Republic. He fought for freedom and democracy and campaigned for a just society. After the Second World War, he was appointed mayor of Berlin and campaigned for the reconstruction of the city. The city of Berlin was marked by the war and the fall of the Berlin Wall in the 1960s and Brandt had a difficult task ahead of him, but he was determined to rebuild Berlin and make it a thriving city.

In the 1960s, Brandt was elected chairman of the SPD and modernized the party. He was committed to social justice and peace and was a visionary who led Germany and Europe into a better future. Under his leadership, the SPD became the strongest party in 1969 and formed a coalition with the FDP. This government implemented important social and political reforms, including the introduction of co-determination in companies and the legalization of abortion.

Brandt was a great statesman and a courageous fighter for freedom and justice. His legacy lives on to this day and he remains an inspiration to many people who are fighting for a better world. Further information on Willy Brandt can be found at https://de.wikipedia.org/wiki/Willy_Brandt.

Brandt was a man of vision and ideals. He advocated the policy of détente and promoted relations between East and West. His commitment to peace earned him the Nobel Peace Prize in 1971.

Overall, Willy Brandt was a great statesman and an important figure in German political history. His role in the SPD was crucial for the modernization and renewal of the party.

• 4.4 Willy Brandt: Ostpolitik and International Relations

Willy Brandt was an important German politician and Chancellor of the Federal Republic of Germany from 1969 to 1974. Brandt was known for his policy of détente and reconciliation, especially towards the Warsaw Pact countries. In this context, Brandt introduced a new Ostpolitik, which was also referred to as "change through rapprochement". The aim of this policy was to improve relations between the Federal Republic of Germany and the Warsaw Pact countries, in particular relations with Poland and the Soviet Union.

Brandt's Ostpolitik was an important contribution to the policy of détente during the Cold War and contributed significantly to the improvement of international relations. Through his policy of dialogue and cooperation, Brandt was able to help resolve conflicts and build bridges between East and West. Its aim was to improve relations between the Federal Republic of Germany and the Warsaw Pact countries and thus to secure peace in Europe.

Brandt recognized that the path to détente could only be achieved by reducing mistrust and building trust. He advocated a policy based on dialogue and cooperation. Brandt's visit to Warsaw and his kneeling gesture in 1970 symbolized his desire for reconciliation and peace.

The successes of Brandt's Ostpolitik were undeniable. The signing of the Moscow Treaty and the Warsaw Treaty in 1970 and the signing of the Basic Treaty between the Federal Republic of Germany and the GDR in 1972 were important milestones in the history of German relations.

Brandt's Ostpolitik had also played an important role in the preparations for the Helsinki Summit in 1975. This summit led to the signing of the Helsinki Final Act, which enshrined the principles of cooperation and security in Europe.

Brandt's Ostpolitik was an important step on the way to overcoming the Cold War and creating a more peaceful world. We should remember Brandt's legacy and continue to advocate a policy of dialogue and cooperation.

Further information on Willy Brandt's Ostpolitik can be found under the following link: https://de.wikipedia.org/wiki/Ostpolitik

• 4.5 Willy Brandt: Resignation and controversies

In German history, there have been few political figures who have been as polarizing as Willy Brandt. Brandt, once a leader of the SPD and later chancellor, had a long and controversial career in German politics.

One of the most famous moments of Brandt's tenure as Chancellor was his resignation in 1974. His resignation was the result of an espionage affair in which a close collaborator of Brandt was unmasked as an East German spy. Although Brandt himself was not involved in the affair, he took responsibility for it and resigned.

Brandt, however, was not only known for his resignation. During his tenure as Chancellor, he advocated a policy of détente during the Cold War and was an important architect of the Eastern Treaties. These treaties were controversial and led to fierce controversy within Germany and beyond.

The Eastern Treaties were a series of treaties between West Germany and East Germany negotiated by Brandt's government in the 1970s. The aim of the treaties was to normalize relations between the two states and reduce tensions between East and West. The treaties were hailed by many as a historic breakthrough that paved the way for further détente.

However, the Eastern Treaties were also controversial. Some criticized them as unilateral concessions to the GDR, which had done nothing to end its human rights abuses and repression of the opposition. Others argued that the treaties were a necessary step to improve relations between the two German states and reduce the threat of war.

Whatever one's position on the Eastern Treaties, Brandt's role in their creation and implementation cannot be underestimated. He was a courageous and determined leader who worked for a peaceful solution to the conflicts of the Cold War. His legacy as Chancellor will forever be linked to the policy of détente and the Eastern Treaties.

Despite the controversies, Brandt remains an important figure in German history and a symbol of change in Germany. His legacy remains relevant to this day and there are many people who are inspired by his vision of an open and tolerant society.

Here[2] you can find more information about Willy Brandt and his political career.

---

2. https://de.wikipedia.org/wiki/Willy_Brandt

Chapter 5: Helmut Schmidt (1974-1982)

- **5.1 Helmut Schmidt: Biography - Insights into the life of the former German Chancellor**

Helmut Schmidt was one of the most important German politicians of the 20th century. He was born in Hamburg on December 23, 1918 and died in his hometown on November 10, 2015. Schmidt was Chancellor of the Federal Republic of Germany from 1974 to 1982, during which time he played a key role in shaping German domestic and foreign policy.

Helmut Schmidt, born on 23 December 1918 in Hamburg, was a German politician of the SPD and the fifth Chancellor of the Federal Republic of Germany from 1974 to 1982.

Schmidt began his political career in the SPD and became a member of the Bundestag in 1961. In his political career, he held numerous offices, including the office of Federal Minister of Economics from 1967 to 1969 and the office of Federal Minister of Defense from 1969 to 1972.

After the resignation of Chancellor Willy Brandt in 1974, Schmidt was elected chancellor candidate by the SPD and subsequently elected Chancellor by the Bundestag. During his term of office, he campaigned, among other things, for the policy of détente and the strengthening of German-French relations.

Schmidt was also active as a publicist and author and published several books on political and social issues. He was a man with a sharp mind and an independent spirit who was actively involved in German politics and society until his death on November 10, 2015.

During his term of office, Schmidt implemented numerous reforms and advocated strong European integration. He is particularly remembered for his decisive actions during the terrorist attacks of the German Autumn in 1977. Schmidt was considered a tough but fair politician and was also highly regarded internationally.

If you would like to learn more about the life and work of Helmut Schmidt, we recommend the official website of the Helmut and Loki Schmidt Foundation: https://www.helmut-schmidt.de/

• 5.2 Helmut Schmidt: The election as Chancellor

Helmut Schmidt was one of the most important politicians of the post-war period in Germany. His tenure as Chancellor from 1974 to 1982 was marked by political challenges and economic changes.

In the 1976 election for Federal Chancellor, Helmut Schmidt ran against the candidate of the CDU, Helmut Kohl. The election campaign was fiercely contested and marked by political controversy. In the end, Helmut Schmidt prevailed with a narrow majority and was able to continue his work as Chancellor.

Helmut Schmidt's political career was impressive and marked by numerous successes. As Chancellor of the Federal Republic of Germany, he advocated the strengthening of the democratic rule of law and the social market economy. But his political career began much earlier: as Minister of Defence and Minister of Finance, he was able to gain valuable experience and expand his political network.

But that's not all: Helmut Schmidt was also active in various international bodies and campaigned for European integration. Among other things, he was a member of the European Parliament and the European Council. His vision of a united and strong Europe still endures today, and his political ideas have had a significant impact on European politics.

However, Helmut Schmidt was not only a successful politician, but also an important intellectual. His numerous books and essays testify to a sharp mind and a deep understanding of political contexts. In addition, he was a great lover of music and was also committed to the promotion of young talents as a patron.

All in all, Helmut Schmidt was a personality who left his mark on many areas of public life. His political legacy is still of great importance today and his ideas will continue to inspire many people in the future.

However, Helmut Schmidt's political career was not without controversy. In particular, his stance on nuclear power and NATO policy caused discussion and criticism. Nevertheless, he remains one of the most important politicians in German history who worked for the stability and progress of Germany.

More information about Helmut Schmidt and his political career can be found on the official website of the Federal Government: www.bundesregierung.de.

• 5.3 Helmut Schmidt: The role in his party (SPD)

Helmut Schmidt was an important politician who had a significant influence on the Social Democratic Party of Germany (SPD). He was Chancellor from 1974 to 1982 and was considered one of the most prominent figures in post-war German politics.

Schmidt was a man with clear ideas and a strong sense of responsibility. He had an impressive career in the SPD and held many important positions before becoming Chancellor. In doing so, he repeatedly demonstrated his ability to master difficult situations and make smart decisions.

Helmut Schmidt played a prominent role in the SPD as a pioneer and strategist. His clear language and unwavering determination to work for a socially just society made him one of the most important politicians of the post-war period. Schmidt was a man whose word counted and who always showed a clear edge when it came to standing up for his convictions.

In addition to his political beliefs, Schmidt was also an advocate of dialogue with other parties. He recognized that cooperation and a search for majorities for important reforms were necessary to achieve change in society.

A list of his most important speeches and writings can be found on the official website of the Federal Chancellor Helmut Schmidt Foundation.

The importance of Helmut Schmidt for the SPD and German politics as a whole can hardly be overestimated. His legacy continues to have an impact today and is an important part of German history.

If you want to know more about Helmut Schmidt and his role in the SPD, I recommend the official website of the SPD: https://www.spd.de/geschichte/personen/helmut-schmidt/.

• 5.4 Helmut Schmidt: Economic and Social Policy

Helmut Schmidt, the fifth Chancellor of the Federal Republic of Germany, was an important political actor of his time. As a member of the Social Democratic Party of Germany (SPD), he had a strong influence on the country's economic and social policy.

During his time in office, Schmidt carried out important reforms that changed Germany permanently. One of the reforms was the introduction of unemployment benefits. This reform made it possible for people who became unemployed to receive financial assistance. Another important reform was the promotion of social housing. Schmidt understood that affordable housing is a basic need for all people and that the state has a responsibility to ensure this.

In addition, Schmidt played an important role in the modernization of the German economy. He promoted innovation and technology and recognized the need to put Germany's economy on a modern, efficient and competitive footing. These reforms have contributed to Germany's leading role in the global economy today.

Schmidt was also a strong proponent of European integration. He recognized that the future of Germany was closely intertwined with the future of Europe and that cooperation between European countries was crucial. Schmidt advocated greater cooperation and integration between European countries, and his vision was an important foundation for today's European Union.

All in all, Schmidt was a great statesman who had a lasting impact on Germany and Europe. His legacy will be remembered for a long time and his reforms have improved the lives of many people.

In a time of political change and economic uncertainty, Helmut Schmidt was a strong and determined leader who stood up for the interests of Germany and Europe. His political decisions and legacy continue to have an impact on German politics and European integration to this day.

Further information on Helmut Schmidt and his political career can be found at: https://www.bundeskanzler-helmut-schmidt.de/

5.5 Helmut Schmidt: Challenges and Deselection – A Look Back at the Political Career of the Former Federal Chancellor

Helmut Schmidt, the former Chancellor of the Federal Republic of Germany, was one of the most influential political figures of the post-war period. As Chancellor from 1974 to 1982, he faced many challenges, both nationally and internationally. During this time, he had to deal with questions of economics, security policy and international relations.

One of the biggest challenges Schmidt faced was the oil crisis in the 1970s. This crisis led to a global recession and posed enormous problems for Germany's economy. Schmidt responded with a series of measures that helped to overcome the crisis and get the German economy back on track.

Despite his successes as chancellor, Helmut Schmidt was voted out of office by his own coalition partner, the FDP, in 1982. This election was a turning point in Helmut Schmidt's political career and marked the end of an era in German politics.

Many people were surprised by this decision, as Schmidt was considered one of the most influential politicians in Germany. During his tenure, he advocated for a strong economy, a liberal society, and a peaceful foreign policy. His decisions were often controversial, but he still enjoyed a high level of respect and recognition.

Although Schmidt was no longer politically active, he continued to be an important part of public life. He was involved in various social and cultural projects and regularly gave interviews on current political issues.

Even after his death in 2015, Helmut Schmidt remains an important figure in German history. His contributions to German politics and society will be remembered for a long time to come.

Today we remember Helmut Schmidt as a great statesman and an important figure in the history of Germany. His legacy will stay with us for a long time to come, reminding us that we must always be ready to face life's challenges.

Capitel 6: Helmut Kohl (1982-1998)

• 6.1 Helmut Kohl: Biography - A Life for Politics

The biography of Helmut Kohl is undoubtedly a fascinating read for anyone interested in the history of the Federal Republic of Germany. Kohl, who came from the Palatinate as a young man, has moved and left a lot behind in his long career as a politician.

Kohl's political career began in the 1960s as a member of the state parliament of Rhineland-Palatinate. After taking over the leadership of the CDU in 1973, he was elected Chancellor in 1982. Kohl's tenure as Chancellor of the Federal Republic of Germany lasted until 1998.

Kohl's life and work are inextricably linked to German history. For example, he played an important role in the reunification of Germany in 1990. The introduction of the euro as the common currency of European countries is also an important milestone in Kohl's political career.

The biography of Helmut Kohl is thus not only an exciting portrait of one of the most important German politicians of the post-war period, but also an important contribution to the political history of Germany and Europe. If you want to learn more about Kohl's life and work, you should not miss this fascinating read.

As Chancellor of Unity, Helmut Kohl reunited the German nation and advanced European integration. His influence on the political landscape of Germany and Europe is undeniable and his political decisions have affected the lives of millions of people.

During his tenure as Chancellor of Germany, Helmut Kohl made many important decisions that continue to have an impact on German and European politics today. Among other things, he introduced the euro as a common currency in Europe. Kohl's vision of a united Europe has contributed to the perception of Europe today as a political and economic power on the world stage.

But Kohl's political influence extends far beyond Europe. His understanding of democracy and cooperation between nations helped Germany play an important role in international politics after the end of the Cold War. Kohl's tireless commitment to German reunification also contributed to the reunification of East and West Germany after years of separation.

Helmut Kohl's political legacy will be remembered for a long time. His vision of a united Europe and a strong German nation will continue to inspire and influence many people in the future.

This biography is a tribute to the man who dedicated his life to politics. It shows how Kohl grew as a person and politician and how he developed from a young man from a humble background to one of Germany's most important statesmen.

Further information on the biography of Helmut Kohl can be found at: https://www.amazon.de/Helmut-Kohl-Biografie-Hans-Peter-Schwarz/dp/3608945813

• 6.2 Helmut Kohl: The election as Chancellor

Helmut Kohl was a German politician and Chancellor of the Federal Republic of Germany from 1982 to 1998. During this time, he played a key role in driving German reunification forward and getting it off the ground. Kohl was also instrumental in shaping the European Union and advocated close cooperation between European states.

The election of Chancellor in 1990 was a decisive moment in Kohl's career. After the reunification of Germany, he was elected Chancellor by a large majority of the Bundestag. Kohl used this opportunity to further promote the reunification of Germany and to promote close cooperation in Europe.

Kohl's policy of reunification of Germany was a milestone in the history of Germany and Europe. With his vision of a "flourishing landscape" for the former GDR, he advocated a rapid economic integration of the two German states. However, this policy was not without criticism, especially from West German citizens, who feared that their tax dollars would be used to rebuild the East.

Despite the challenges, Kohl remained undeterred and continued to advocate reunification. It became a symbol of hope and unity for people throughout Germany. His leadership skills and commitment to European integration helped him to be regarded throughout Europe as one of the most important statesmen of his time.

Kohl was also a strong supporter of European unification. He was an important architect of the Maastricht Treaty and promoted the creation of a common currency, which later became known as the euro. His commitment to European integration and cooperation contributed to his being remembered as one of Europe's most important statesmen.

Overall, Kohl's political career was marked by many successes, but also by challenges and criticism. However, his legacy as chancellor and European statesman will endure and serve as an inspiration for future generations.

Kohl has also experienced some controversy in his career, especially in connection with the party donation scandal in the 1990s. Nevertheless, he remains an important figure in German and European history.

Further information on the election of Helmut Kohl as Federal Chancellor can be found here: https://www.bundesarchiv.de/DE/Content/Artikel/Artikel-ausserhalb-der-Navigation/Personen-Geschichte/Kohl-Helmut/kohl-helmut.html

• 6.3 Helmut Kohl: The role in his party (CDU) and his legacy

Helmut Kohl will go down in history as one of Germany's most important politicians. He decisively shaped the fate of the Federal Republic of Germany for many decades and, as Chancellor from 1982 to 1998, promoted German unity. His work has had a significant impact not only on German but also on European history.

Kohl was a visionary who worked for a strong and united European Union. His political career began at a young age and eventually led him to the top of the Federal Republic of Germany. During his tenure as Chancellor, he advocated for the reunification of Germany and worked closely with other European leaders to advance European integration.

Even in difficult times, Kohl has proven time and again that he was a great statesman. His legacy will endure long after his death, and his ideas will continue to inspire many people in the future.

If you would like to learn more about Helmut Kohl, please visit the official website of the Konrad Adenauer Foundation: https://www.kas.de/de/themen/dossier-helmut-kohl.

But Helmut Kohl played an important role not only in federal politics, but also in his party, the CDU. He was federal chairman of the CDU from 1973 to 1998 and had a strong influence on the party during this time. Under his leadership, the CDU has won many election victories and pushed through important reforms.

Even after his death in 2017, Helmut Kohl remains an important part of German history and a role model for many politicians. His legacy will live on and inspire future generations as well. Kohl was one of the most influential politicians of the post-war period and made a significant contribution to the reunification of Germany. His political career and achievements have been honoured in numerous books, articles and documentaries.

Kohl was a man of great stature and charisma. His leadership skills and political prowess were unparalleled. During his tenure as Chancellor of Germany, he made many important decisions that had a lasting impact on the country. His vision of a united Europe and his role in the introduction of the euro have resonated not only in Germany, but also in Europe as a whole.

Even after his death, Kohl remains an important point of reference for politicians. His legacy will live on and inspire future generations as well. Kohl has shown that it is possible to have a clear vision even in difficult times and to implement it successfully. His legacy will be with us for a long time to come, reminding us that a strong Europe can only be achieved through cooperation and solidarity.

Here's a URL to an article about Helmut Kohl's political legacy: https://www.bundeskanzler-helmut-kohl.de/politisches-erbe/

More information about Helmut Kohl and his role in German politics can be found at the following link: https://de.wikipedia.org/wiki/Helmut_Kohl

6.4 Helmut Kohl: German Unity and European Integration

Helmut Kohl, the sixteenth Chancellor of the Federal Republic of Germany, was one of the most important statesmen in German history. A special feature of his term of office was the reunification of Germany in 1990. Kohl played a crucial role in this historic event and worked for the creation of a common identity between East and West Germany.

In addition, Helmut Kohl was a passionate advocate of European integration. He recognized early on that the future of Germany and Europe was closely intertwined and worked tirelessly for greater cooperation within the European Union.

Kohl's vision of a united Europe endures to this day and has helped the EU become one of the most powerful political and economic forces in the world. Under his leadership, important steps have been taken towards closer cooperation and integration, such as the introduction of the euro as a common currency.

Even today, many people remember Kohl's services to European unification and his commitment to a peaceful future for the continent. His legacy remains unforgotten and will continue to play an important role in shaping and developing Europe in the future.

More information about Helmut Kohl and his political career can be found on the official website of the Konrad Adenauer Foundation: https://www.kas.de/de/web/geschichte-der-cdu/personen/biogramm-detail/-/content/helmut-kohl-3.

6.5 Helmut Kohl: Controversial Issues and Donation Scandal

Helmut Kohl, the Chancellor of the Federal Republic of Germany from 1982 to 1998, was one of the most influential figures in German post-war history. During his tenure, he has raised many controversial issues and championed his beliefs.

However, Helmut Kohl's term of office was also overshadowed by the so-called "donation affair". In 1999, Kohl publicly admitted that he had accepted illegal party donations during his time in office. This affair had a serious impact on his political legacy and his reputation as a statesman.

The "donation affair" was a profound scandal in German politics that dragged on for years and led to a deep crisis of confidence among the population. The illegal acceptance of party donations was a serious violation of the German Political Parties Act and shook the German political landscape permanently.

The scandal affected not only Helmut Kohl, but also other prominent politicians and parties. The investigation and clarification of the affair dragged on for years, and it took a long time for the public to be fully informed about the illegal activities.

The consequences were far-reaching: Helmut Kohl was fined, and other politicians also had to answer for their crimes. The "donation affair" was a sad chapter in the history of German politics and has permanently shaken the public's confidence in the integrity and morality of politicians.

More information about the "donation affair" can be found under the following link: https://de.wikipedia.org/wiki/Spendenaffäre_der_CDUCSU

Nevertheless, Kohl remains an important figure in German history. As Chancellor of German reunification, he made a decisive contribution to the unity of Germany, and his role in European integration should not be underestimated.

For more information on the political life of Helmut Kohl, you can visit the following link: https://www.bundeskanzler-helmut-kohl.de/

Further information on his career and the controversy surrounding Helmut Kohl can be found at the following link: https://de.wikipedia.org/wiki/Helmut_Kohl.

Chapter 7: Gerhard Schröder (1998-2005)

• 7.1 Gerhard Schröder: Biography - A Life Full of Political Ups and Downs

Gerhard Schröder is one of the most important political personalities of post-war Germany. During his term of office from 1998 to 2005, the former Chancellor introduced important reforms and campaigned for greater European integration.

Gerhard Schröder was born on April 7, 1944 in Mossenberg-Wöhren, a small town in Lower Saxony. After graduating from high school, he studied law at the universities of Göttingen and Hamburg. Schroeder began his political career as a member of the Social Democratic Party (SPD). In 1978 he was elected as the youngest Minister-President in the history of Lower Saxony and held this office until 1990.

In 1998, the greatest success of his political career followed: Schröder was elected Chancellor of the Federal Republic of Germany. During his term of office, he campaigned, among other things, for a reform of the labour market and the social system. Schroeder also played an important role at the international level, especially in connection with the Iraq war in 2003.

Despite his political successes, there was also criticism of Schroeder. In particular, his proximity to business and his work as a lobbyist after the end of his term as Chancellor were criticized by many.

More information about Gerhard Schröder and his political career can be found on the official website of the Federal Government: https://www.bundesregierung.de/breg-de/bundeskanzlerin-und-bundesregierung/fruehere-bundeskanzler-und-bundespraesidenten/gerhard-schroeder

During his tenure as Chancellor, Gerhard Schröder pushed through important reforms, such as Agenda 2010, which included labour market reforms in Germany. He has also advocated greater European integration and nurtured relations with the United States.

Despite his political successes, Gerhard Schröder also suffered some setbacks. Particularly controversial was his decision to involve Germany in the Iraq war. After losing the 2005 federal election, he resigned from all political offices and switched to business.

Today, Gerhard Schröder works as an advisor and speaker and advocates for better cooperation between Germany and Russia. You can read more about his life and political career on his official website: https://www.gerhard-schroeder.de/

• 7.2 Gerhard Schröder: The election as Chancellor

The election of Gerhard Schröder as Chancellor in 1998 was a significant moment in German history. As the first chancellor of the red-green coalition, Schroeder had the difficult task of leading Germany in a time of economic upheaval and international uncertainty.

However, Schroeder had a clear vision for Germany's future and advocated reforms that would help modernize the economy and prepare the country for the challenges of the 21st century. His reforms led to fierce debates and protests, but ultimately they helped make Germany one of the most competitive countries in the world.

Under Schroeder's leadership, numerous reforms were implemented that had a positive impact on Germany's economy. One of the most significant reforms was Agenda 2010, which provided for a more flexible labour market and a reform of social security systems. These reforms were controversial, but they helped to revive the labour market and modernise social security in Germany.

Schroeder was also a strong supporter of the European Union and advocated closer cooperation within Europe. He worked closely with other European leaders to advance European integration and prepare the EU for global challenges.

Although Schroeder's tenure was not free of controversy, he is considered one of the most influential chancellors in Germany's recent history. His reforms helped make Germany one of the most competitive countries in the world and set the country up for a prosperous future.

Although Schroeder was also criticized in later years, his election as Chancellor remains an important milestone in German history. If you want to know more about this period, you can read more here: https://de.wikipedia.org/wiki/Gerhard_Schr%C3%B6der#Bundeskanzler.

• 7.3 Gerhard Schröder: The role in his party (SPD)

Gerhard Schröder, former German Chancellor and member of the Social Democratic Party of Germany (SPD), has taken on many roles in his long political career. Schroeder was one of the most important and influential politicians of his time and left a lasting impression on German politics.

Schroeder joined the SPD in 1963 and quickly climbed the political ladder. He was a member of the Bundestag and later Minister-President of Lower Saxony. He was elected Chancellor in 1998 and led Germany through many important events such as the introduction of the euro and the reform of the labour market.

During his time as a member of the SPD, Gerhard Schröder played a controversial role in his party. Some critics accused him of being too pro-business and focusing too much on Agenda 2010, which disappointed many Social Democratic voters. But it is also undeniable that Schroeder was able to push through economic reforms and lead Germany through difficult times.

Under Schroeder's government, unemployment in Germany was reduced and the economy strengthened. He championed an agenda that focused on privatizing state-owned enterprises, deregulating labor markets, and cutting taxes on corporations. However, these measures were not without controversy and led to protests and criticism.

Overall, however, Schroeder is regarded as one of the most significant figures in German politics in recent decades. His ability to push through economic reforms and lead Germany through difficult times is considered by many to be remarkable. And although he also had to take criticism, Schroeder's influence on German politics and business remains noticeable to this day.

Today, Schroeder is no longer active in the SPD, but he remains an important figure in German politics and business. He has founded a consulting firm and is active in many international organizations. Despite the controversies surrounding his political role, Schroeder remains a fascinating figure who has had a lasting impact on German politics and society.

Source: https://de.wikipedia.org/wiki/Gerhard_Schröder[1]

• *7.4 Gerhard Schröder: Agenda 2010 and economic reforms*

Gerhard Schröder was the seventh Chancellor of the Federal Republic of Germany from 1998 to 2005. One of his most important policy initiatives was Agenda 2010, a comprehensive reform programme aimed at making the German economy more competitive and modernising social security systems. The program included changes in labor and social law, tax cuts, and investments in education and infrastructure.

Although Agenda 2010 was seen by many as a necessary step towards modernising the German economy, it was also met with fierce resistance. Some argued that the reforms were at the expense of workers and exacerbated social inequality. Others criticized Schroeder for working too closely with big business and neglecting the interests of the workers.

Nevertheless, there are also supporters of Agenda 2010. They argue that it has helped make Germany more competitive and reduce unemployment. Agenda 2010 has also helped to restore investor confidence in the German economy.

---

1. https://de.wikipedia.org/wiki/Gerhard_Schr%C3%B6der

However, it is undeniable that Agenda 2010 had a profound impact on German society. Many people lost their jobs and had to settle for precarious employment. It is important to analyse the impact of Agenda 2010 on German society to ensure that future reforms are fair and equitable.

Whatever one's position on Schroeder's political agenda, it is indisputable that he had a significant influence on German politics and the economy. Today, he is often regarded as one of the most controversial figures in post-war German history.

Here is a link to more information about Gerhard Schroeder and his political agenda: https://de.wikipedia.org/wiki/Gerhard_Schröder

• 7.5 Gerhard Schröder: International Politics and Criticism

Gerhard Schröder is undoubtedly one of the most influential figures in German politics in recent decades. As a former Chancellor, he has made a large number of decisions that have influenced political events in Germany and Europe. But Schroeder also plays an important role in international politics.

In this context, it is interesting to deal with Schroeder's criticism of the policies of other countries. In the past, Schroeder has repeatedly commented on issues such as U.S. foreign policy and Germany's role in the European Union. In doing so, it has often triggered controversial debates and polarized.

One of Schroeder's best-known speeches came in February 2003, when he spoke out clearly against the Iraq war and explicitly advised Germany not to participate. This speech was very controversial both in Germany and internationally. Schroeder was denounced by some as an "anti-American," while others praised him for his courage and clear stance.

Schroeder has also repeatedly taken clear positions on other issues. For example, he has spoken out in favour of strengthening the European Union and has spoken out against nationalist tendencies. At the same time, he has repeatedly emphasised that Germany bears a special responsibility for the future of Europe.

Overall, Schroeder's political legacy remains controversial. While some praise him as one of Germany's most important chancellors, others accuse him of having done too little to prepare the country for the challenges of the 21st century. Nevertheless, Schroeder's influence on German politics and society remains undisputed.

If you are interested in Schroeder's political views and positions, you can find an extensive collection of articles and speeches by the former Chancellor on the website of the Friedrich Ebert Foundation (https://www.fes.de/themenportal-publikationen/internationale-politik-und-gesellschaft/gerhard-schroeder).
These offer a deep insight into Schroeder's political thinking and his view of international politics.

Chapter 8: Angela Merkel (2005-2021)

• 8.1 Angela Merkel: biography

Angela Merkel, born on 17 July 1954 in Hamburg, is one of Germany's best-known political figures. Merkel grew up in East Germany and studied physics before entering politics.

In 1990, Angela Merkel entered the political arena and has since become one of Germany's most influential women. Their influence on German politics and the European Union is undisputed.

Merkel has overcome many challenges during her term in office and has proven herself to be a strong leader. During her tenure as Chancellor, she advocated for greater cooperation within Europe and played an important role in overcoming the European debt crisis.

In recent years, Merkel has also had to deal with the refugee crisis. She has worked for a humanitarian solution and called on the German people to stand together in these difficult times.

Merkel has also made a name for herself internationally and is an important mediator in international conflicts. She has worked for a peaceful and diplomatic solution to conflicts and has repeatedly campaigned for the observance of human rights and democratic values.

Angela Merkel has achieved a lot during her term of office as Chancellor and steered Germany safely through difficult times. She will be remembered as one of the most influential women in the history of Germany.

Source: https://www.bundeskanzlerin.de/bkin-de

Merkel has also played an important role in international politics and has been one of the most important voices in the European Union. She has worked to strengthen German-American relations and to comply with the Paris Climate Agreement.

Merkel's biography is an inspiring story of perseverance, determination, and leadership. Their influence on German politics and the world will continue for a long time to come. If you want to know more about Angela Merkel's life and career, please visit the official website of the German government: https://www.bundesregierung.de/breg-de/bundeskanzlerin/bundeskanzlerin-angela-merkel.

• 8.2 Angela Merkel: The election as Chancellor

Angela Merkel, Germany's first female chancellor, has left a lasting mark on the political landscape of her country and Europe. Since taking office in 2005, she has steered the fortunes of Germany and Europe through turbulent times, proving time and time again that she is one of the world's most capable leaders.

The election as Chancellor in 2005 was a historic moment for Germany. Angela Merkel, who previously served as Minister for the Environment, Nature Conservation and Nuclear Safety, prevailed in a contest against then-Chancellor Gerhard Schröder. Since then, she has won four more terms and is considered one of the most influential politicians in the world.

During her time in office, Angela Merkel has overcome many challenges and made important decisions that have had a lasting impact on Germany and Europe. It initiated the energy transition and decided to phase out nuclear power, which has put Germany on a greener and more sustainable path. It has also played a crucial role in overcoming the euro crisis and has advocated for close cooperation within the European Union.

But her chancellorship was not always without controversy. In particular, her decision to open the borders to refugees during the refugee crisis in 2015 has provoked a lot of criticism and led to a political split in Germany. However, Merkel has always advocated a humanitarian solution and European solidarity.

Despite all the challenges and criticism, Angela Merkel has had a lasting impact on German politics and society and will undoubtedly go down in Germany's history as one of the most important chancellors. For more information on Angela Merkel's chancellorship, please visit the official website of the German government: https://www.bundesregierung.de/breg-de/bundeskanzlerin

Merkel's political style is often described as pragmatic and unagitated. She has managed to stabilize Germany's economy and lead the country through difficult times such as the financial crisis and the refugee crisis. In doing so, she has repeatedly emphasized that she is committed to a strong, united Europe.

Take a look at this page[1] for more information about Angela Merkel and her work as Chancellor.

• 8.3 Angela Merkel: The role in her party (CDU)

Angela Merkel is one of the most influential women in the world and has achieved many successes in her political career. She has been Chancellor of Germany since 2005 and has played a key role in shaping the country's political landscape. But what about her role in her own party, the Christian Democratic Union (CDU)?

Merkel has many friends and supporters in her party, but also some critics. Some members of the CDU accuse her of being too liberal and not conservative enough. Others praise her for her pragmatic and forward-looking policies.

Despite the criticism Angela Merkel receives from within her own party, she has many admirers in the German and international political landscape. Merkel has proven to be a strong and reliable leader, especially during the euro crisis and the refugee crisis. Its policy of dialogue and cooperation has contributed to a stable and prosperous European Union.

Another reason for Merkel's success is her ability to adapt to a changing world. She has dealt intensively with the challenges of digitalization and developed a vision for the digital future of Germany and Europe. Merkel has also taken a global leadership role in tackling climate change and advocated for a sustainable and environmentally friendly future.

It is important to emphasize that Merkel's political successes are not without criticism. There are also some who question their decisions and their political agenda. But it is undeniable that Merkel is one of the most influential and successful political figures of our time.

---

1. https://www.bundeskanzlerin.de/bkin-de

Despite these disagreements, Merkel has successfully led the CDU through difficult times and strengthened her position as chancellor. She has modernized the party and given it a new, more open image. Merkel is a strong and respected leader who also enjoys great international recognition.

More information on Angela Merkel's role in her party (CDU) can be found on the official website of the Christian Democratic Union (CDU): https://www.cdu.de/angela-merkel

• 8.4 Angela Merkel: Energy policy and the euro crisis

Angela Merkel is undoubtedly one of Germany's best-known politicians and has been Germany's Chancellor since 2005. In her long political career, she has overcome many challenges and has proven herself time and again as a strong and competent leader.

One of its biggest challenges was undoubtedly overcoming the euro crisis that shook Europe between 2009 and 2012. Merkel was faced with the difficult task of finding a solution that satisfied all the countries of the European Union. She advocated for a common European solution and worked hard to stabilise the economy within the EU. Thanks to their commitment and determination, the crisis was finally overcome.

Merkel is also known for her role as an important mediator in international conflicts. She has repeatedly advocated for a peaceful solution to conflicts and has proven herself as a diplomat even in difficult situations. Her ability to make difficult decisions while always keeping the well-being of Germany and Europe in mind has made her one of the most important political figures of our time.

You can find out more about Angela Merkel and her political career here: https://www.bundeskanzlerin.de/bkin-de

Another important issue that Merkel has tackled during her term in office is energy policy. Here, she campaigned for an energy transition and promoted the expansion of renewable energies such as wind and solar energy. These measures helped reduce Germany's dependence on fossil fuels and protect the environment.

Merkel's political activities and decisions have often sparked controversial discussions. Some critics accuse her of not doing enough to combat social inequalities in Germany. Others praise her leadership and determination in difficult times.

Overall, Angela Merkel has undoubtedly exerted a strong influence on German politics and the European Union. Their vision of a united Europe and a sustainable energy policy will continue to inspire many people.

8.5 Angela Merkel: Refugee crisis and her leadership role

Angela Merkel played a crucial leadership role in the 2015 refugee crisis. Their decision to open the borders to refugees was a bold move, but it also drew criticism.

When Angela Merkel decided in 2015 to take in refugees from Syria and other countries, the decision sparked a fierce debate in Germany and around the world. Many people saw Merkel's decision as a humanitarian gesture in line with Germany's tradition of hospitality. In the past, Germany has often taken in refugees and offered them a new home.

Others, on the other hand, criticized that the decision would lead to an increase in crime and an overload of the German social system. This criticism was amplified by some politicians and the media, which led to a split in society.

Despite the controversies and challenges associated with the decision, Germany has made efforts to integrate the refugees and give them a chance at a better life. Numerous initiatives have been launched to help refugees integrate and develop their skills and talents.

The debate about the refugee crisis in Germany is far from over. But it is important that we continue to strive to create an open and tolerant society in which all people have equal opportunities, regardless of their origin or background.

Nevertheless, Merkel stood by her decision and advocated a European solution to the refugee crisis. She called for solidarity from other European countries and stressed the importance of a common European refugee policy.

Merkel's leadership in the refugee crisis has provoked both admiration and criticism. But regardless of one's opinion of her decisions, there is no denying that Merkel has taken responsibility for Germany and Europe at a difficult time.

More information on the refugee crisis and Merkel's role can be found here[2].

---

2. https://www.bundeskanzlerin.de/bkin-de/themen/fluechtlingskrise

Chapter 9: Olaf Scholz (since 2021)

• 9.1 Olaf Scholz: Biography - From Hamburg Senator of the Interior to Chancellor Candidate

Olaf Scholz is one of Germany's best-known and most experienced politicians and is currently the SPD's candidate for chancellor. Born in Osnabrück, he was born in 1958 and grew up in Hamburg. After graduating from high school, he studied law and **then worked** as a lawyer.

He began his political career in the SPD, where he quickly rose through the ranks and was appointed Senator of the Interior of Hamburg in 2001. Scholz has held many important offices in his political career, including the positions of First Mayor of Hamburg, Deputy Federal Chairman of the SPD and Federal Minister of Finance.

During his time as First Mayor of Hamburg, Scholz was instrumental in the Hanseatic city's bid to host the 2024 Olympic Games. In addition, he campaigned for the modernisation of the Port of Hamburg and the expansion of local public transport.

Scholz is also a convinced European and is committed to a strong European Union that is capable of acting. He called for closer cooperation in the eurozone and a reform of the European Union.

As the SPD's candidate for chancellor, Scholz advocates socially just policies that put people at the centre. He advocates higher taxation of wealth and a strengthening of the welfare state.

In this position, Scholz advocated for effective policing and a safe city. Among other things, he founded the special unit MEK and campaigned for the expansion of video surveillance. In 2007, he was elected First Mayor of Hamburg and held this office until 2018.

As finance minister in the grand coalition from 2018 to 2021, Olaf Scholz played a crucial role in overcoming the Corona pandemic and saving Lufthansa. During his tenure, he has proven that he is an experienced crisis manager and acts quickly when it counts.

When the coronavirus pandemic broke out in 2020, Olaf Scholz was at the forefront and worked tirelessly to minimize the economic damage. He was instrumental in developing the stimulus package that helped keep the economy moving and jobs secured.

Olaf Scholz also showed his skill in rescuing Lufthansa. The airline had been put in a difficult position by the pandemic and was in danger of collapsing. Olaf Scholz campaigned for the German government to provide Lufthansa with financial support in order to save the company from insolvency.

Olaf Scholz is regarded as a man of action who acts quickly and decisively in difficult situations. His experience and commitment have earned him respect and recognition in politics and among the population.

With his candidacy for chancellor in the 2021 Bundestag election, Olaf Scholz wants to pave the way for a fairer, more supportive and more sustainable society. His political goals include fair taxation of the rich, a strong social policy and a consistent climate policy.

Here is the link to Olaf Scholz's official website: https://www.olafscholz.de/biografie/

•9.2 Olaf Scholz: The election as Chancellor and his political goals

. Olaf Scholz was elected as the new Chancellor of the Federal Republic of Germany on Wednesday, 8 December 2021. In the Bundestag, the SPD MP received 395 out of 707 votes cast in the 20th legislative period (2021 to 2025), with 369 votes required for the election. In the secret ballot with concealed voting cards, there were 303 votes against, six abstentions, and three votes invalid.

At the beginning of the plenary session, Bundestag President Bärbel Bas read out the letter from Federal President Dr. Frank-Walter Steinmeier, who had proposed Olaf Scholz for election as Federal Chancellor in accordance with Article 63 (1) of the Basic Law. Scholz succeeds Dr. Angela Merkel, who has held the office since 2005. After the election, Olaf Scholz was appointed Federal Chancellor by the Federal President at his official residence Schloss Bellevue.

Angela Merkel had only been in office in an acting capacity since 26 October. The MPs, with the exception of the AfD parliamentary group, thanked the outgoing Chancellor with prolonged applause. The election of the new Chancellor took place with concealed ballot papers, and Olaf Scholz needed the Chancellor's majority, i.e. at least 369 votes in the new 736-member Bundestag.

• 9.3 Olaf Scholz: The role in his party (SPD)

Olaf Scholz has been First Mayor of the Free and Hanseatic City of Hamburg since 8 December 2017. Previously, he was Federal Minister of Labour and Social Affairs from 2007 to 2009 and Deputy Federal Chairman of the SPD from 2011 to 2018. Since 6 December 2019, he has also been acting chairman of the SPD.

In the SPD, Scholz is seen as a representative of the right wing and a supporter of a grand coalition with the CDU/CSU. He is one of the party's most influential and well-known politicians and has held several important offices in the past.

More information about Olaf Scholz and his role in the SPD can be found at the following link: https://www.spd.de/partei/personen/olaf-scholz/

• 9.4 Olaf Scholz: Future projects and political agenda

Olaf Scholz is an eminent German politician who currently serves as Chancellor. In recent years, he has been involved in many important future projects and political issues. Scholz was instrumental in introducing the minimum wage, which is an important improvement for many workers in Germany.

Another important issue Scholz is working on is the reform of the European Union. Scholz has spoken out in favour of making the EU more democratic and transparent and strengthening cooperation between member states. He also supports the idea of a European army to increase security in Europe.

As a former First Mayor of Hamburg, Scholz also has a lot of experience in urban development. He has been committed to sustainable and environmentally friendly urban planning and is also committed to climate protection at the national level.

Scholz is an important political actor in Germany and Europe and is committed to many important issues that can improve people's lives. More information about Olaf Scholz and his political projects can be found on his official website: https://www.olafscholz.de/.

• 9.5 Olaf Scholz: Early Challenges and Public Perception

Olaf Scholz, the former First Mayor of Hamburg and current Chancellor of the Federal Republic of Germany, has overcome many challenges in his political career. Scholz has been active in German politics for many years and has gained a reputation as a competent and assertive politician during this time.

As mayor of Hamburg, Scholz had to deal with a number of crises. One of the biggest challenges was undoubtedly the Hamburg G20 summit in 2017, which was accompanied by massive protests. In these difficult times, Scholz showed himself to be a level-headed and strong politician who knew how to keep calm and keep the situation under control.

But Scholz has proven that he is an experienced and competent politician not only in times of crisis. During his tenure as First Mayor of Hamburg, he has launched numerous projects that have improved the lives of the city's citizens. For example, he has promoted the expansion of local public transport and campaigned for climate protection.

At the federal level, Scholz has also taken important decisions in his function as Federal Minister of Finance to strengthen the German economy and promote social cohesion. Among other things, he has launched a historic economic stimulus package to cushion the effects of the coronavirus pandemic.

It is clear that Scholz is an experienced and competent politician who can keep a cool head even in difficult times. We are fortunate to have such a politician in our ranks.

As Federal Minister of Finance, Olaf Scholz has done an outstanding job in recent years and has been instrumental in leading the German economy through difficult times. During the COVID-19 pandemic in particular, Scholz acted quickly and decisively to cushion the financial impact of the crisis and stabilise the economy.

Under his leadership, significant financial assistance was launched to mitigate the impact of the pandemic on businesses and workers. Scholz has always advocated a fair and fair distribution of financial support, thus sending a strong signal of solidarity in society.

Thanks to his experience and competence, Scholz has been able to contribute to Germany's comparatively good position during the crisis and has also received international recognition for its measures. His commitment to stabilising the economy has thus proved indispensable.

More information about Olaf Scholz and his work as Federal Minister of Finance can be found on the official website of the Federal Ministry of Finance: https://www.bundesfinanzministerium.de/Weitere   Themen/Politik/ Bundesregierung/olaf-scholz.html

Despite his successes, Scholz has also faced criticism. In particular, the Federal Minister of Finance came under criticism with regard to his role in the-ex tax affair. However, Scholz has always emphasized that he bears no responsibility for the questionable business practices and has campaigned for a comprehensive investigation into the affair.

Overall, Olaf Scholz is an experienced and respected politician who has overcome many challenges in his career. Although he is not free from criticism, he is appreciated by many people in Germany for his ability to handle difficult situations and make smart decisions.

Closing remarks

This book provides a comprehensive overview of the Chancellors of the Federal Republic of Germany since their inception. It sheds light on general aspects such as the tasks of the Federal Chancellor, the electoral process and political contexts during the elections. Each chapter is dedicated to a Federal Chancellor and contains information on biography, election, role in the party, political decisions and points of criticism.

It is important to emphasize that this book aims to provide objective information and does not reflect the opinions of the author or the publisher. The facts presented are for the sole purpose of providing a historical overview. Any political interpretation or condemnation is avoided and it is made clear that the book assumes no liability for political content.

The focus is on the presentation of events and developments in the context of the respective terms of office of the Federal Chancellors in order to provide readers with a well-founded insight into Germany's political history.

JAN DRIESSEN

Imprint:

Jan Dierssen

Hammersbecker Weg 6

28790 Schwanewede

buecherjan1993@gmail.com